GREAT YARMOUTH · I

CAISTER-ON-SEA · HOPTON ON SEA

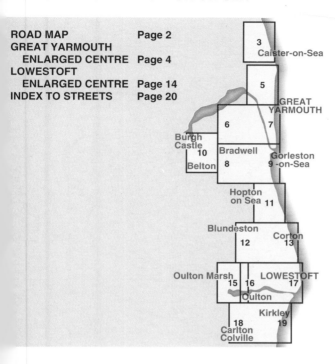

Every effort has been made to verify the accuracy of information in this book but the publishers cannot accept responsibility for expense or loss caused by an error or omission. Information that will be of assistance to the user of the maps will be welcomed.

The representation on these maps of a road, track or path is no evidence of the existence of a right of way.

Car Park	P
Public Convenience	C
Place of Worship	+
One-way Street	→
Pedestrianized	▨
Post Office	●

Scale of street plans 4 inches to 1 mile
Unless otherwise stated

eet plans prepared and published by ESTATE PUBLICATIONS, Bridewell House, TENTERDEN, KENT.
The Publishers acknowledge the co-operation of the local authorities
of towns represented in this atlas.

Ordnance Survey® This product includes mapping data licensed from Ordnance Survey®
with the permission of the Controller of Her Majesty's Stationery Office.

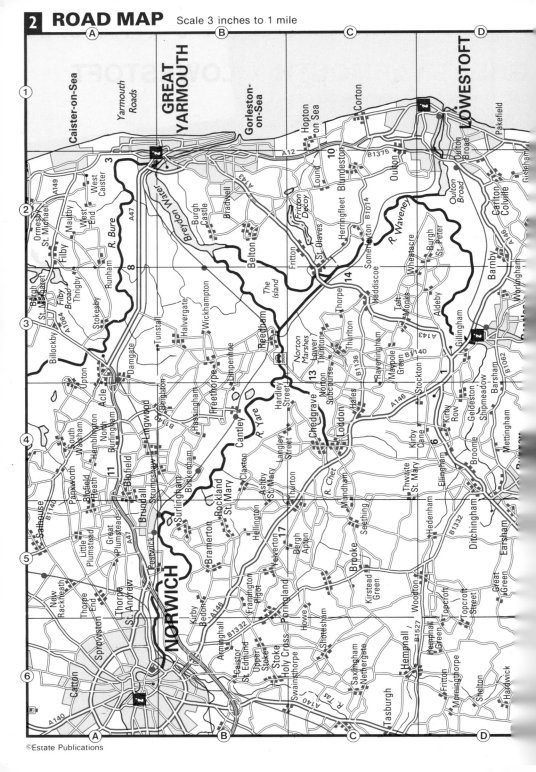

2 ROAD MAP Scale 3 inches to 1 mile

©Estate Publications

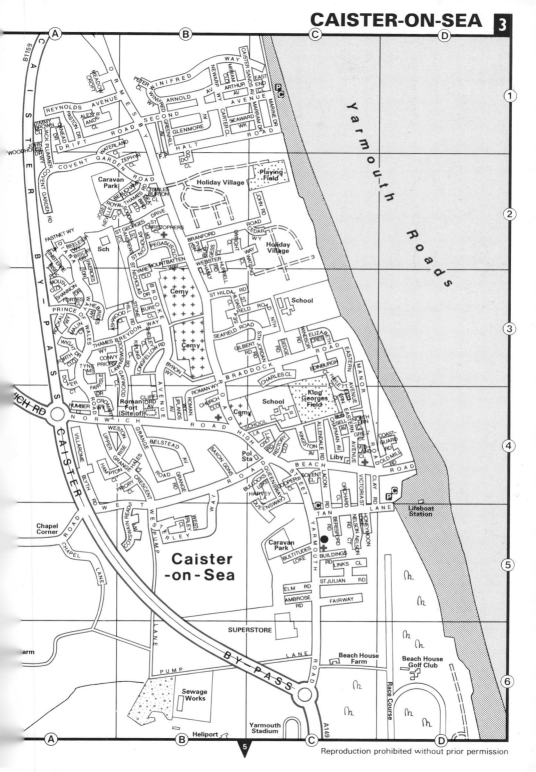

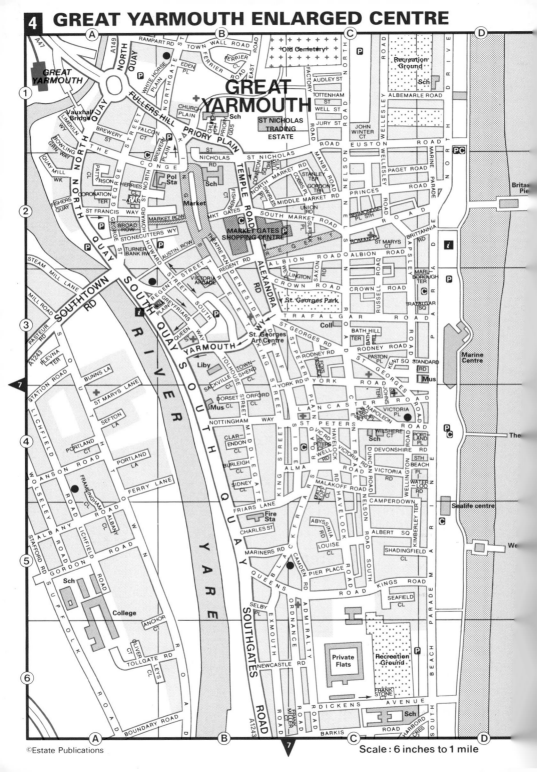

4 GREAT YARMOUTH ENLARGED CENTRE

Scale : 6 inches to 1 mile

©Estate Publications

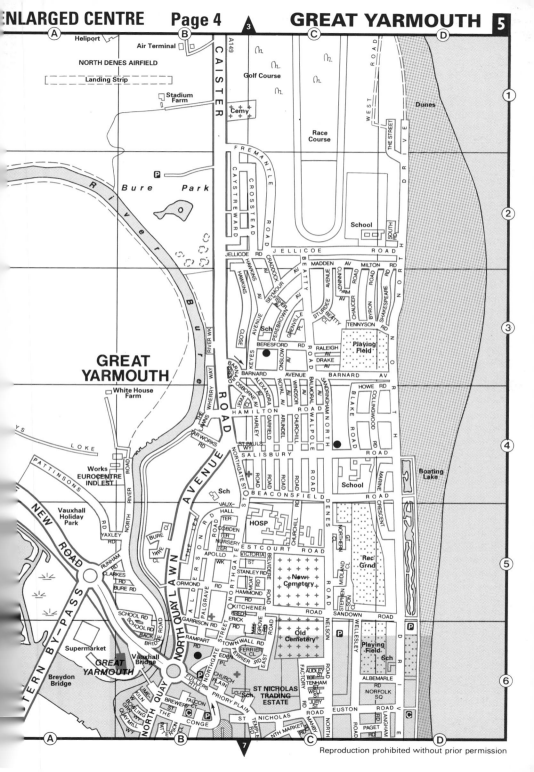

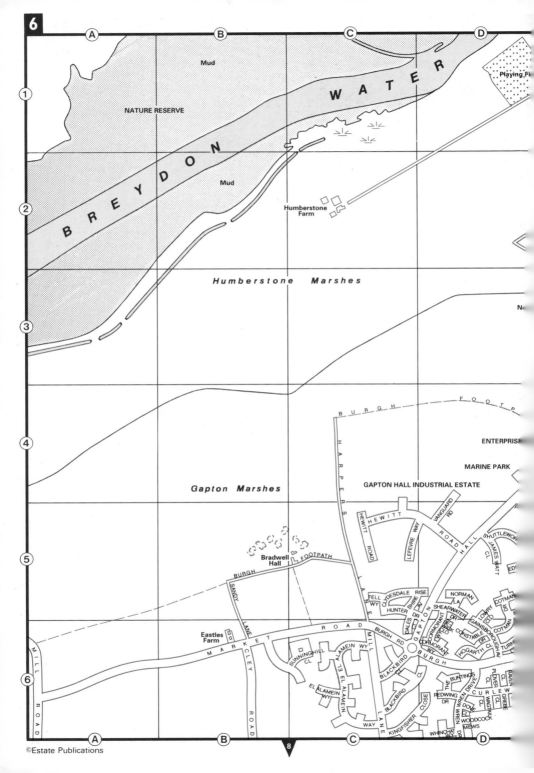

6

BREYDON WATER

Mud

NATURE RESERVE

Mud

Playing Fi

Humberstone Farm

Humberstone Marshes

N

BURGH FOOTP

ENTERPRIS

MARINE PARK

Gapton Marshes

GAPTON HALL INDUSTRIAL ESTATE

HARPERS

HEWITT

HEWITT ROAD

VANGUARD RD

LEFEVRE WAY

ROAD HALL

SHUTTLEWO

JAMES WATT CL.

ED

Bradwell Hall

FOOTPATH

BURGH

SANDY

NORMAN LA

COTMAN

FELL WY

CLOESDALE RISE

SHIRE DR

HUNTER

DALES DR

GAPTON

SHEARWATER

CORMORANT

LOWRY CL

GAINSBOROUGH AV

CONSTABLE DR

COTMN

TURNE

Eastles Farm

MILL

LANE

ACKLEY

MARKET ROAD

BURGH ROAD

MILL WY

BURGH RD

GAPTON

CORMORANT

BURGH

HOGARTH CL

RAEB

GREBE

Bradwell Hall

SUNNINGHILL CL

EL ALAMEIN WY

BLACKBIRD CL

KINGFISHER CLOSE

THE BUNTINGS

WREN DRIVE

REDWING DR

DOVE

WAGTAIL CL

CURLEW CL

PLOVER CL

WOODCOCK MEWS

EL ALAMEIN WY

EL ALAMEIN WY

ROAD

BLACKBIRD CL

WREN DR

WHINCHAT CL

MILL ROAD

WAY

8

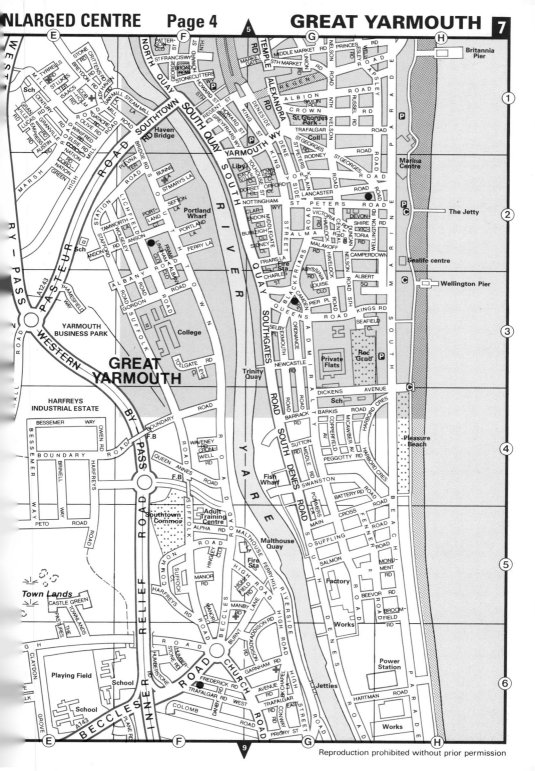

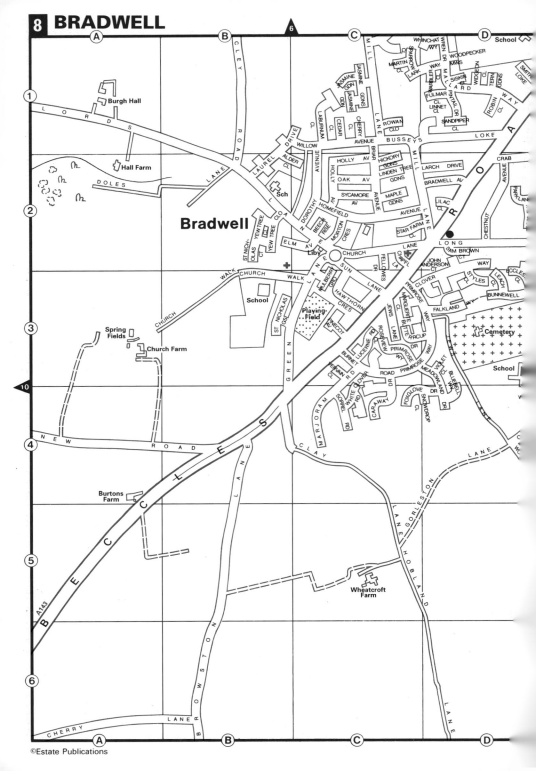

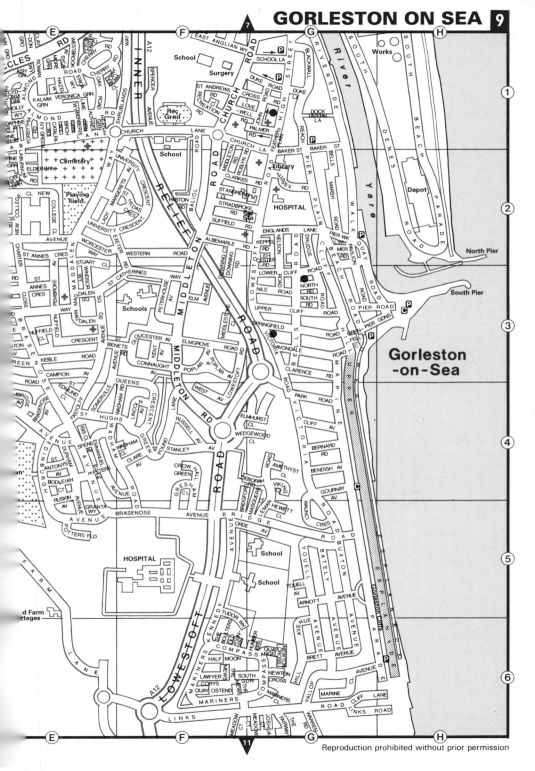

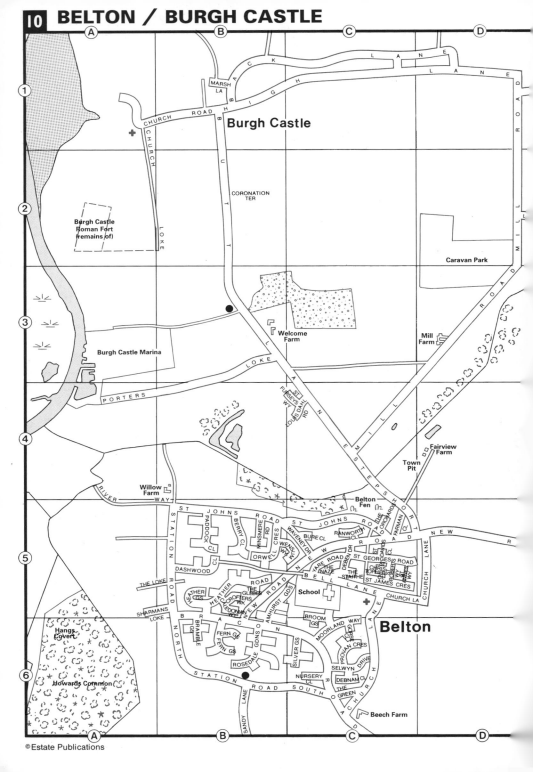

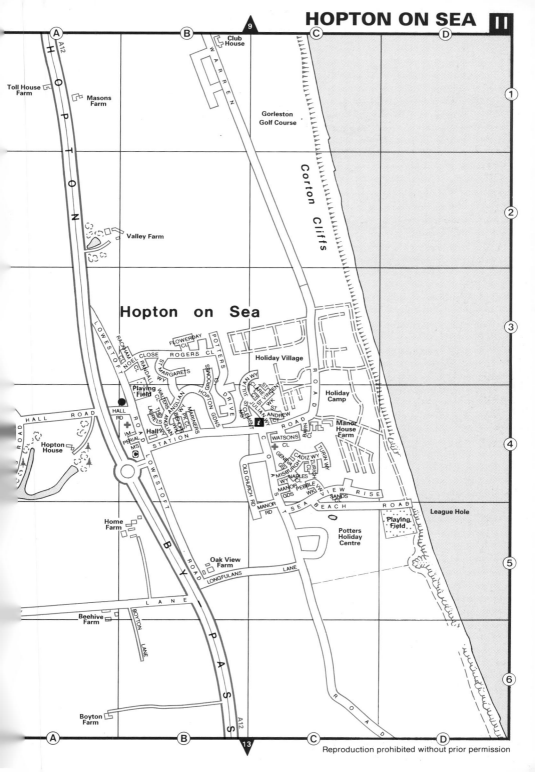

Club House

Gorleston Golf Course

Corton Cliffs

Toll House Farm

Masons Farm

Valley Farm

Hopton on Sea

HOPTON ROAD
A12
LOWESTOFT ROAD

FLOWERDAY CL
NOEL CL
RACKHAM WY
RANDALL WY
ST MARGARETS
WATERS
THE LAURELS
ANGLIAN
BEECH
PRIOR
MARINERS
SPIXWOOD CL
HOPTON GDNS
POTTERS CL
ROGERS CL
CLOSE

Holiday Village
Holiday Camp

Playing Field

HALL ROAD
ROAD
HALL RD
IM-PERIAL
MS
Hall
STATION
ROAD
C
Hopton House

ALAN WY
LANE
ST VINCENT
ST
JULIAN
ST HERBERT
ST ANDREW
WK
ROAD

Manor House Farm

WATSONS CL
GENISTA
MISBURGH WY
CL
MANOR GDNS
NAPLES CL
PEBBLE WK
CADIZ WY
TURIN WY
TURIN
SANDS
SEA VIEW RISE
ROAD

OLD CHURCH RD
MANOR RD

BEACH ROAD

League Hole

Playing Field

Home Farm

Oak View Farm

Potters Holiday Centre

LANE
LONGFULANS LANE

Beehive Farm

BOYTON LANE

BY PASS ROAD

ROAD

A12

Boyton Farm

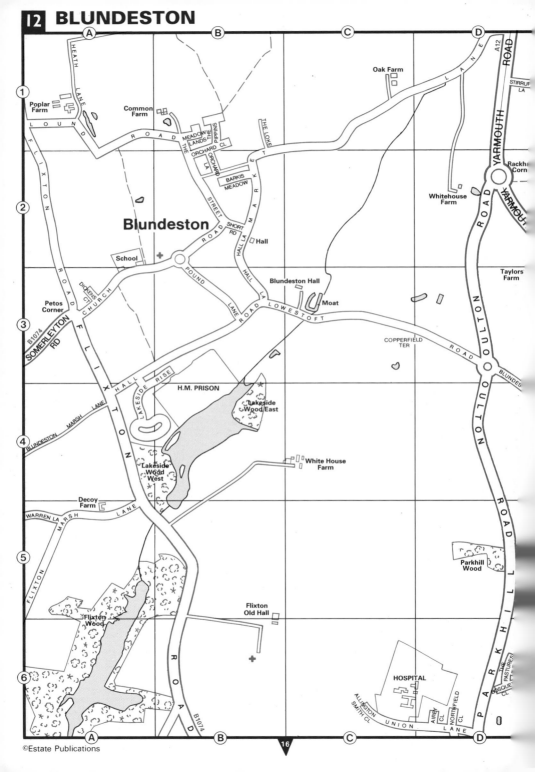

Blundeston

Poplar Farm
Common Farm
Oak Farm
Whitehouse Farm
Rackham Corn
Taylors Farm
School
Petos Corner
Hall
Blundeston Hall
Moat
Copperfield Ter
H.M. PRISON
Lakeside Wood East
Lakeside Wood West
White House Farm
Decoy Farm
Parkhill Wood
Flixton Wood
Flixton Old Hall
HOSPITAL

HEATH LANE
LOUND ROAD
FLIXTON ROAD
MEADOW LANDS
THE ORCHARD
THE PIPPINS
ORCHARD CL
BARKIS MEADOW
STREET
MARKET
HALL LA
THE LOKE
SHORT RD
POUND LANE
HALL ROAD
LOWESTOFT ROAD
LANE
YARMOUTH ROAD
A12
STIRRUP LA
YARMOUTH
OULTON ROAD
BLUNDES
CHURCH
DICKENS
SOMERLEYTON RD
B1074
FLIXTON
MARSH LANE
LAKESIDE RISE
HALL ROAD
BLUNDESTON
WARREN LA
MARSH LANE
FLIXTON
ROAD
B1074
PARKHILL ROAD
THE PASTURES
BISGATE CL
ALLINGTON
SMITH CL
UNION LANE
AIRE CL
NORTHFIELD CL
THE NORTHFIELD

16

©Estate Publications

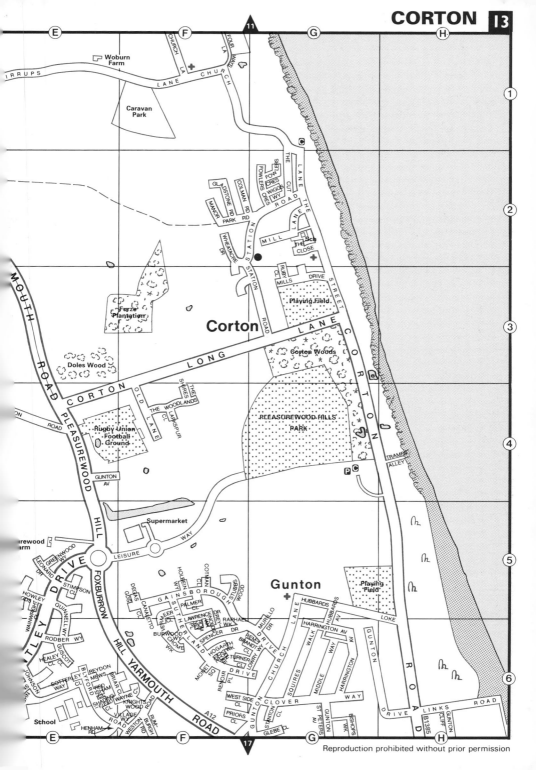

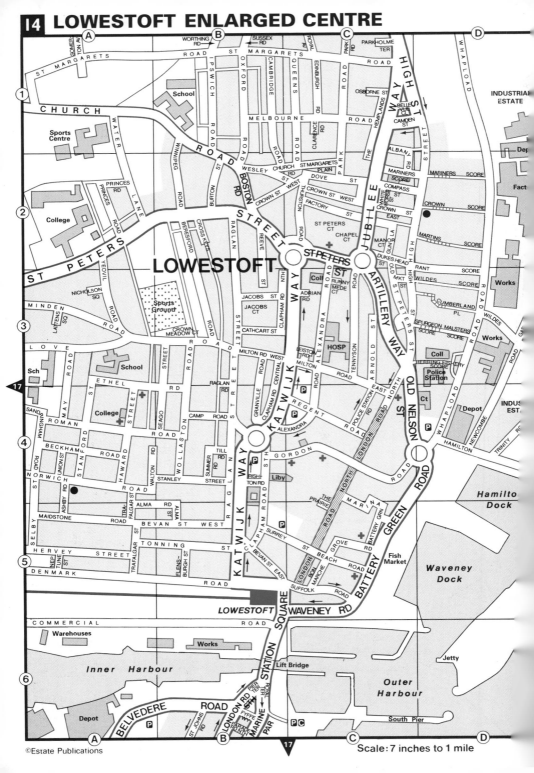

14 LOWESTOFT ENLARGED CENTRE

©Estate Publications

Scale: 7 inches to 1 mile

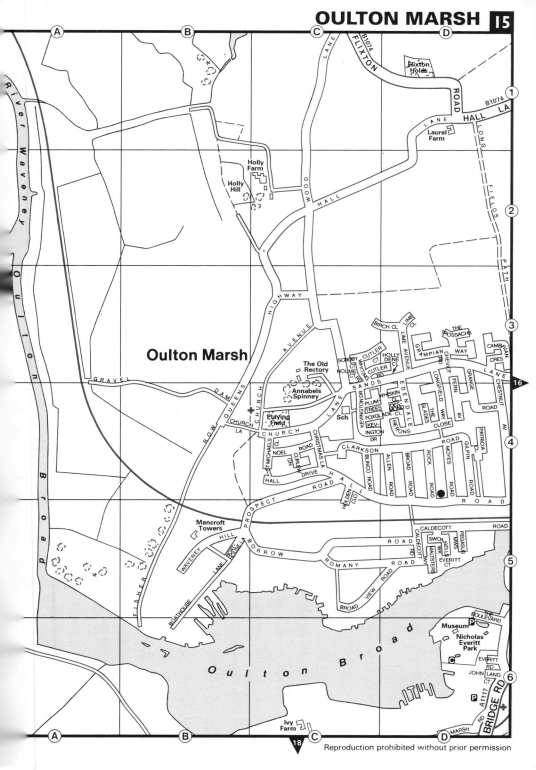

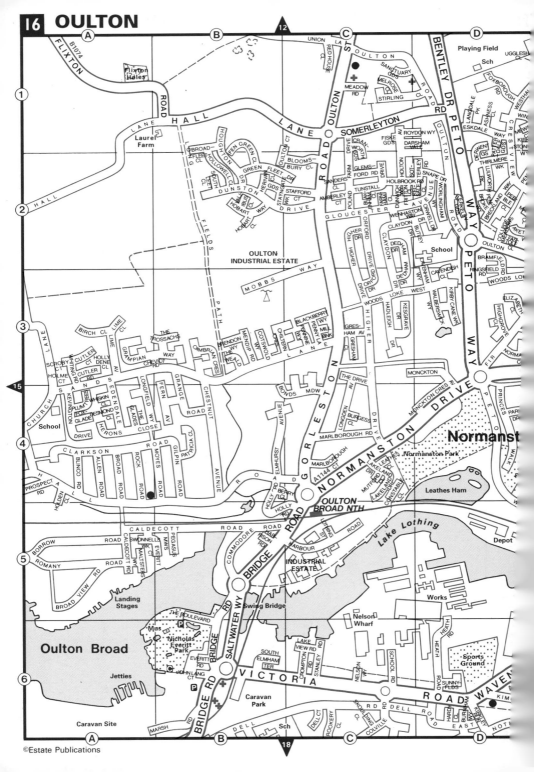

16 OULTON

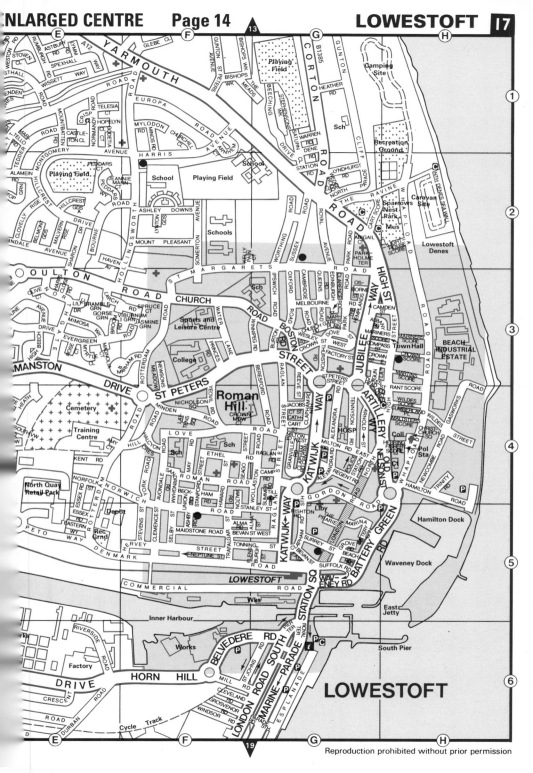

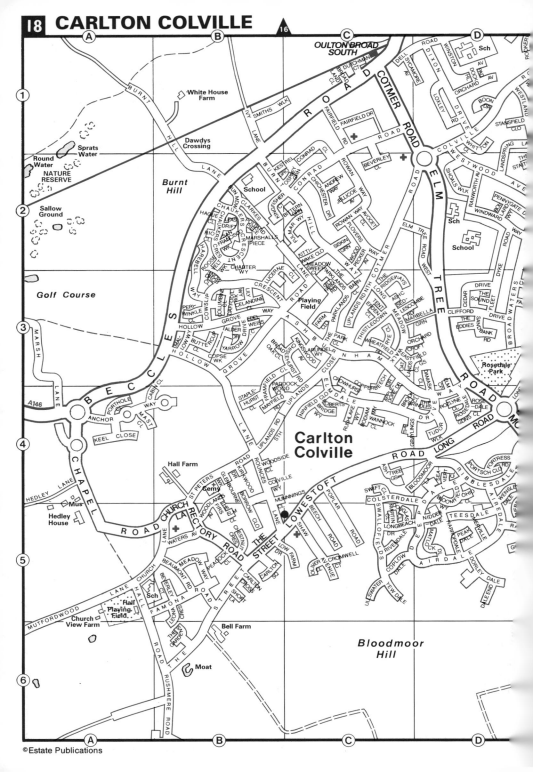

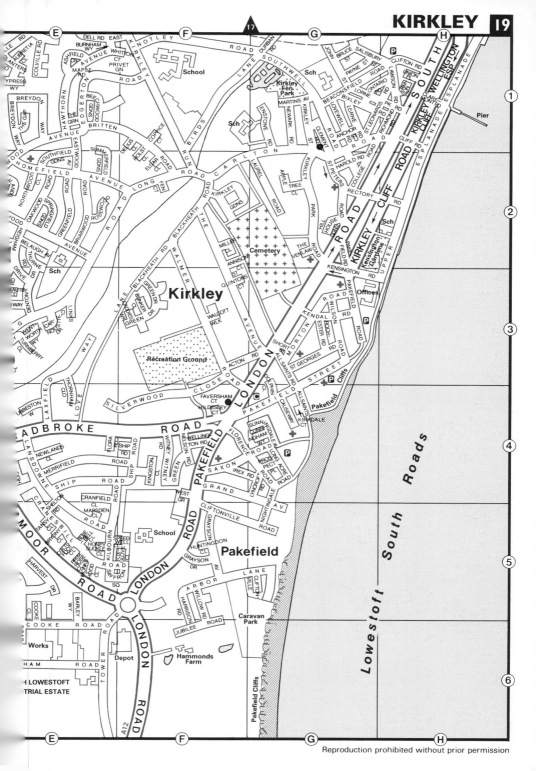

The Index includes some names for which there is insufficient space on the maps. These names are preceded by an * and are followed by the nearest adjoining thoroughfare.

Elmhurst Clo. NR31 9 G4
Isle Rd. NR31 7 E1
Emmanuel Av. NR31 9 E4
Empress Rd. NR31 7 E1
Englands La. NR31 9 G2
Erica Way. NR31 9 E1
Estcourt Rd. NR30 5 C5
Euston Rd. NR31 4 C1
Exeter Rd. NR31 9 F2
Exmouth Rd. NR30 4 B5

Factory Rd. NR30 4 C1
Falcon Ct. NR30 4 C1
Falkland Way. NR31 8 D3
Faraday Rd. NR31 7 E4
Farman Clo. NR31 10 C5
Fastolff Av. NR31 9 E4
Feathers Plain. NR31 9 G1
Fell Way. NR31 6 C5
Fellowes Dri. NR31 8 C2
Fenner Rd. NR30 7 G5
Fern Gdns. NR31 10 B6
Ferrier Clo. NR30 4 B1
Ferrier Rd. NR30 4 B1
Ferry Hill. NR31 7 G5
Ferry La. NR31 4 A4
Fisher Av. NR30 5 C3
Fishers Ct. NR30 4 B2
Fishers Quay. NR30 4 A2
Fizalan Clo. NR30 4 A2
Forsythia Dri. NR31 9 E1
Foxglove Dri. NR31 8 C4
Fox's Pass. NR30 4 C3
Framlingham Clo.
NR31 4 A5
Frank Stone Ct. NR30 4 C6
Frederick Rd. NR30 5 B5
Fremantle Rd. NR30 5 B1
Frederick Rd,
Gorleston. NR31 7 F6
Friars La. NR30 4 B5
Friars Hill. NR30 4 A1
Frimar Clo. NR31 8 D1

Gainsborough Av.
NR31 6 D6
Galton Hall Rd. NR31 7 E4
Garfield Rd. NR31 5 C4
Garnham Rd. NR31 7 G6
Garrison Rd. NR31 5 B5
George cre Rd. NR31 7 E1
George St. NR31 4 A2
Gibson Rd. NR31 9 E3
Gloucester Av. NR31 9 F3
Glenville Rd. NR31 9 E3
Gordon Rd. NR31 4 A5
Gordon Ter. NR30 4 C2
Gorleston La. NR31 8 C5
Grange Clo. NR31 10 C2
Granby Av. NR31 9 G4
Granta Way. NR31 9 E5
Granville Rd. NR31 7 E1
Green, Northern Clo.
NR30 5 C5
Greene Clo. NR31 6 D6
Green La. NR31 8 B3
Greenacres. NR31 8 D4
Greenwell Ct. NR31 9 G3
Greenville Pl. NR31 5 C3
Gresham Clo. NR31 9 F4
Greyfriars Way. NR30 4 B3

Haddon Rd. NR31 9 F6
Hain. NR30 4 B3
Halton Rd. NR30 5 B4
Hammond Rd. NR30 5 B5
Hammond Cres. NR30 7 G4
Harrys Rd. NR31 7 E4
Hart Rd. NR30 5 C4
Hastings La. NR31 6 C4
Hawkins Ct. NR30 4 C6
Heathen Rd. NR30 7 G6
Hemsbeck Rd. NR30 4 C4
Herbs Av. NR30 5 B2
Herbs Clo. NR31 5 B3
Hern Cres. NR31 8 C3
Hern Rd. NR31 9 E1
Herway. NR31 9 E1
Hessington Clo. NR31 8 D2
Hewern. NR31 9 F1
Heyward Gdns. NR31 10 B5
Hextonford Rd. NR31 10 B5
Hextonlo. NR31 6 D6
Hexton Clo. NR30 4 A2
Heywood Way. NR31 9 E3
Heywood Clo. NR31 9 G4

Hewitt Rd. NR31 6 C5
Hickory Gdns. NR31 8 C2
High La. NR31 10 B1
High Mill Rd. NR31 7 E2
High Rd. NR31 7 F5
High St. NR31 9 G1
Highfield Rd. NR31 7 G5
Hill Av. NR31 9 G6
Hingley Clo. NR31 7 F5
Hobland La. NR31 8 C5
Hogarth Clo. NR31 6 D6
Holly Av. NR31 8 C2
Holly Way. NR31 9 E1
Homefield Av. NR31 8 C2
Hornbeam Clo. NR31 9 E1
Howard St Nth. NR30 4 A2
Howard St Sth. NR30 4 A2
Howe Rd. NR31 5 C4
Humber Keel. NR31 9 G6
Humberstone Rd. NR31 7 F6
Hunter Dri. NR31 9 E1

INDUSTRIAL & RETAIL:
Beacon Pk. NR31 9 E6
Enterprise Park.
NR31 6 D4
Eurocentre Ind Est.
NR30 5 A4
Gapton Hall Ind Est.
NR31 6 C4
Gapton Retail Pk.
NR31 7 E3
Harfreys Ind Est.
NR31 7 E4
Marine Park. NR31 6 D4
St Nicholas
Trading Est. NR30 5 C6
Yarmouth Business Pk.
NR31 7 E3
Inner Relief Rd. NR31 7 F6
Isaacs Rd. NR31 7 E1
Isis Clo. NR31 9 E4
Ivy Grn. NR31 9 E1

James Watt Clo. NR31 6 D5
Jasmine Gdns. NR31 8 C1
Jasmine Grn. NR31 9 E1
Jellicoe Rd. NR30 5 B2
Jema Clo. NR30 5 B4
Jews La. NR31 8 C3
John Anderson Ct.
NR31 8 D2
John Rd. NR31 9 G1
John Winter Ct. NR30 4 C1
Johns Av. NR31 9 E3
Johns Ter. NR30 4 C4
Joshua Clo. NR31 9 G6
Jury St. NR30 4 C1

Kalmia Grn. NR31 9 E1
Keble Rd. NR31 9 E1
Kennedy Av. NR31 9 F6
Kent Av. NR31 9 F3
Kent Sq. NR30 4 C3
Keppel Rd. NR31 9 G2
Kestrel Clo. NR31 6 D6
Keyes Av. NR30 5 C3
Kimberley Ter. NR30 4 C5
King St. NR30 4 B1
Kingfisher Clo. NR31 6 C6
Kings Rd. NR30 4 C5
Kings Rd,
Gorleston. NR31 9 E2
Kings Walk. NR31 9 E2
Kitchener Rd. NR30 5 B5

Laburnum Clo. NR31 8 C1
Laburnum Rd. NR31 9 E2
Lady Haven Rd. NR31 7 E1
Lady Margarets Av.
NR31 9 E2
Lancaster Rd. NR30 4 C4
*Lancaster Sq,
York Rd. N30 4 C3
Langham Rd. NR30 5 D6
Lapwing Clo. NR31 6 D6
Larch Dri. NR31 8 D2
Lark Way. NR31 8 D1
Laurel Dri. NR31 8 B2
Lawn Av. NR30 5 B5
Lawyer Corys. NR31 9 F6
Leach Clo. NR31 8 D3
Lefevre Way. NR31 6 C5
Leicester Rd. NR31 9 G2
Leman Rd. NR31 9 G5
Leys Clo. NR31 4 A6

Lichfield Rd. NR31 4 A4
Lilac Clo. NR31 8 D2
Lime Way. NR31 9 E1
*Limekiln Walk,
Limekiln Way. NR30 4 A1
Limekiln Way. NR30 4 A1
Limmer Rd. NR31 9 G2
Lincoln Av. NR31 9 F4
Linden Tree Gdns.
NR31 8 C2
Links Rd. NR31 9 F6
Linnet Clo. NR31 8 D1
Long La. NR31 8 D2
Lords La. NR31 8 D2
Louis Dahl Rd. NR31 10 C4
Louise Clo. NR30 4 C5
Lovewell Rd. NR31 9 F1
Lower Cliiff Rd. NR31 9 G3
Lower Esp. NR31 9 G3
Lowestoft Rd. NR31 9 F6
Lowry Clo. NR31 6 D5
Lucas Rd. NR31 7 E1
Lucerne Rd. NR31 8 C3
Lynn Gro. NR31 7 E6

Madden Av. NR30 5 C2
Magdalen Sq. NR31 9 E3
Magdalen St. NR31 9 E3
Magdalen Way. NR31 9 E3
Main Cross Rd. NR30 7 G5
Malakoff Clo. NR30 4 C4
Malakoff Rd. NR30 4 C4
Mallard Way. NR31 8 D1
Malthouse La. NR31 7 F5
Manby Rd. NR30 4 C2
Manby Rd,
Gorleston. NR31 7 F5
Manor Clo. NR31 7 F5
Manor Rd. NR31 7 F5
Maple Gdns. NR31 8 C2
Marguerite Clo. NR31 8 C3
Marine Clo. NR31 9 G6
Marine Cres. NR30 5 C4
Marine Par. NR30 4 D5
Marine Par,
Gorleston. NR31 9 G3
Mariners Clo. NR31 9 G6
Mariners Compass.
NR31 9 F6
Mariners Rd. NR30 4 B5
Marjoram Rd. NR31 8 C4
Market Gates. NR30 4 B2
Market Rd. NR31 6 B6
Market Row. NR30 4 A2
*Marl Ter,
Crown Rd. NR30 4 C3
Marlborough Ter.
NR30 4 D3
Marsh La. NR31 10 B1
Marsh Rd. NR31 7 E2
Martin Clo. NR31 8 C1
Masquers Clo. NR31 9 G5
*Maud Ter,
Belvidere Rd. NR30 5 C5
Maygrove Rd. NR30 5 C6
Meadow Ct. NR31 9 F6
Meadowland Dri. NR31 8 D3
Merton Av. NR31 9 E1
Micawber Av. NR30 7 G4
Middle Market Rd.
NR30 4 B2
Middle Rd. NR30 7 G4
Middlegate. NR30 4 B4
Middlestone Clo. NR31 9 F3
Middleton Rd. NR31 9 F3
Midland Clo. NR30 5 C5
Mill La. NR31 6 C6
Mill La. NR31 8 C2
Mill Rd. NR31 7 E1
Mill Rd,
Burgh Castle. NR31 10 C4
Mill Rd. NR31 6 A6
Milton Rd. NR31 5 C2
Minsmere Rd. NR31 10 B5
Moat Rd. NR30 5 C5
Monument Rd. NR30 7 H5
Moorland Way. NR30 10 C6
Morton Cres. NR31 8 C2
Morton Peto Rd. NR31 6 D5
Mulberry Gro. NR31 8 C3

Napoleon Pl. NR31 4 C4
Nelson Rd. NR31 9 G2
Nelson Rd Central.
NR30 4 C2
Nelson Rd Nth. NR30 4 C2

Nelson Rd Sth. NR30 4 C5
New College Clo. NR31 9 E2
New Rd. NR31 10 B5
Newcastle Rd. NR30 4 B6
Newnham Grn. NR31 9 E3
Newton Cross. NR31 9 G6
Nile Rd. NR31 9 G3
Norfolk Sq. NR30 5 C6
Norman La. NR31 6 D5
North Denes Rd. NR30 5 C4
North Dri. NR30 4 D2
North Market Rd.
NR30 4 B2
North Quay. NR30 4 A2
North River Rd. NR30 5 B5
North Rd. NR31 9 G3
Northgate St. NR30 5 B4
Nottingham Way.
NR30 5 B4
Nuffield Cres. NR31 9 E3
Nuffield Clo. NR31 9 E3
Nursery Rd. NR31 10 C6
Nursery Ter. NR30 5 B5

Oak Av. NR31 8 C2
Oak Rd. NR31 9 E1
Old Fountain. NR31 9 F6
Old Wellington Pl,
Duncan Rd. NR30 4 C4
Olive Rd. NR31 7 E1
Oliver Ct. NR31 4 A6
Onslow Av. NR30 5 C3
Orde Av. NR31 9 F5
Orford Clo. NR30 4 B4
Oriel Av. NR31 8 D4
Oriel Way. NR31 9 E4
Ormond Rd. NR30 5 B5
Orwell Cres. NR31 10 B5
Osborne Av. NR30 5 B4
Owen Rd. NR31 7 E4
Oxford Av. NR31 9 E4

Paddock Clo. NR31 10 B5
Paddys Loke. NR30 5 A4
Paget Rd. NR30 4 C2
Palgrave Rd. NR30 5 B5
Palmer Rd. NR31 9 G1
Park Rd. NR31 9 G4
Parkland Dri. NR31 8 D2
Pasteur Rd. NR31 7 E3
Paston Pl. NR30 4 C3
Paston Rd. NR30 9 F2
Patterson Clo. NR30 4 A2
Pattinsons Rd. NR30 5 A4
Pavilion Rd. NR31 9 G2
Peggotty Rd. NR30 7 G4
Pembroke Av. NR31 9 E3
Perebrown Av. NR30 5 C3
Peterhouse Av. NR31 9 F3
Pier Gdns. NR31 9 G3
Pier Pl. NR30 4 C5
Pier Plain. NR31 9 G2
Pier Rd. NR31 9 G3
Pier Walk. NR31 9 G2
Pinbetts La. NR31 9 E2
Pinecot Av. NR31 8 C3
Pintail Dri. NR31 8 D1
Plane Rd. NR31 7 F6
Plevna Ter. NR31 4 A3
Plover Clo. NR31 6 D6
Pommers La. NR31 7 G5
Poplar Av. NR31 9 F3
Porters Loke. NR31 10 A4
Portland Clo. NR31 4 A4
Portland La. NR31 4 A4
Portland Pl. NR30 4 C4
Potters Field. NR31 9 E5
Pound La. NR31 9 F4
Primrose Way. NR31 8 C3
Princes Rd. NR30 4 C2
Priory Gdns. NR30 4 B1
Priory Plain. NR30 4 B1
Priory St. NR31 7 G6
Provan Clo. NR31 10 C6

Quay Angel. NR30 9 G6
Quay Mill Walk. NR30 4 A2
Quay Ostend. NR31 9 F6
Quay Rd. NR31 9 G2
Queen Annes Rd.
NR31 7 F4
Queen St. NR30 4 B3
Queens Cres. NR31 9 F3
Queens Rd. NR30 4 B5
*Queens Sq,
Albion Rd. NR30 4 C2

Raleigh Av. NR30 5 C3
Rambouillet Clo. NR31 8 D2
Rampart Rd. NR30 5 B6
Ranworth Clo. NR31 10 C5
Raven Clo. NR31 6 D6
Recreation Clo. NR31 9 F1
Recreation Rd. NR31 9 F1
Redwing Dri. NR31 6 D6
Regent Rd. NR30 4 B2
Regent St. NR30 4 A3
River Walk. NR30 5 B3
River Way. NR31 10 A4
Riverside Rd. NR31 7 G5
Riverside Walk. NR31 9 G1
Robin Clo. NR31 8 D1
Rodney Rd. NR30 4 C3
Roman Pl. NR30 4 C2
Rosedale Gdns. NR31 10 B6
Roseview Clo. NR31 8 C3
Roslyn Rd. NR31 9 F2
Rowan Clo. NR31 8 C1
Rowan Way. NR31 9 E1
Royal Av. NR30 5 C3
Runham Rd. NR30 5 A5
Ruskin Av. NR31 9 E4
Russell Av. NR31 9 F4
Russell Rd. NR30 4 C3

Sackville Clo. NR30 4 B3
St Andrews Clo. NR31 9 F2
St Andrews Rd. NR31 9 F1
St Annes Cres. NR31 9 E2
St Annes Rd. NR31 9 E3
St Annes Way. NR31 10 C5
St Antonys Av. NR31 9 E4
St Benets Rd. NR31 9 E3
St Catherines Way.
NR31 9 E3
St Christopher Clo.
NR31 10 C5
St Davids Clo. NR31 10 C5
St Edmund Clo. NR31 9 E4
St Francis Way. NR30 4 A2
St Furseys Way.
NR31 10 C4
*St Georges Pl,
King St. NR30 4 B3
St Georges Rd. NR30 4 C3
St Georges Rd,
Belton. NR31 10 C5
St Hildas Cres. NR31 9 F2
St Hughs Grn. NR31 9 E4
St James Cres. NR31 10 C5
*St James Walk,
York Rd. NR30 4 C3
St Johns Rd. NR31 10 B5
St Lukes Ter. NR31 7 E1
St Marys Ct. NR30 4 C2
St Marys La. NR31 4 A4
St Nicholas Clo. NR31 8 B2
St Nicholas Gdns.
NR31 8 B3
St Nicholas Rd. NR30 4 B2
St Pauls Way. NR30 5 B4
St Peters Av. NR31 9 E4
St Peters Ct. NR30 4 C4
St Peters Plain. NR31 4 C3
St Peters Rd. NR30 4 C4
St Roberts Way.
NR31 10 C5
Salisbury Rd. NR30 5 C4
Salmon Rd. NR30 7 G5
Sam Brown Ct. NR31 8 D2
Sandown Rd. NR30 5 C5
Sandpiper Clo. NR31 8 D1
Sandringham Av.
NR30 5 C3
Sandy La,
Belton. NR31 10 B6
Sandy La,
Bradwell. NR31 6 B5
*Sarah Martin Row,
Howard St. NR30 4 A2
Sawmill La. NR31 7 E1
Saxon Rd. NR31 4 C3
School La. NR31 9 G1
School Rd. NR30 5 B5
School Rd Back. NR31 5 B6
Seafield Clo. NR30 4 C5
Seawake Clo. NR31 9 E2
Sefton La. NR31 4 A4
Selby Pl. NR30 4 B5
Selwyn Dri. NR31 10 C6
Selwyn Rd. NR31 8 D2
Seymour Av. NR31 5 C3

HOPTON-ON-SEA

LOWESTOFT

Cranford Clo. NR33 — 19 E4
Cranleigh Rd. NR33 — 19 E4
Cranworth Gdns. NR32 — 16 C2
Crestview Dri. NR32 — 16 D2
Crisp Clo. NR32 — 17 E1
Crompton Rd. NR33 — 16 C6
Crome Walk. NR32 — 13 F6
Cromwell Ct. NR33 — 18 C5
Cross Keys. NR32 — 14 B2
Crowhurst Clo. NR33 — 18 C3
Crown Meadow Ct. NR32 — 14 B3
Crown Score. NR32 — 14 D2
Crown St East. NR32 — 14 C2
Crown St West. NR32 — 18 C3
Culzean Gdns. NR32 — 16 D1
Cumberland Pl. NR32 — 14 D3
Cunningham Way. NR33 — 19 G4
Curlew Grn. NR32 — 15 C4
Cutler Ct. NR32 — 15 C3
Cutler Rd. NR32 — 15 C3
Cypress Way. NR33 — 19 E1

Daffodil Wk. NR33 — 18 B3
Dale End. NR33 — 18 D5
Damask Clo. NR33 — 18 C3
Danson Ct. NR33 — 19 H1
Dersham Vale. NR32 — 16 C1
Dobham Dri. NR32 — 16 C2
Deepdale. NR33 — 18 D5
Douglas Gdns. NR32 — 13 F5
Derus Clo. NR33 — 19 F1
Denmark Ct. NR33 — 16 C6
Denmark Rd. NR33 — 16 B6
Denmark Rd East. NR33 — 16 C6
Dene Rd. NR32 — 17 G1
Denmark Rd. NR32 — 14 A5
Denton Dri. NR33 — 19 E3
Derwent Gdns. NR32 — 16 D2
Desmond Clo. NR32 — 15 D4
Dickens Ct. NR32 — 12 A3
Dixon Dri. NR33 — 18 D1
Dolphin Clo. NR33 — 19 G4
Dovey Dale. NR33 — 18 D5
Douglas Clo. NR33 — 18 C5
Dove St. NR32 — 14 C2
Dovedale. NR33 — 18 D4
Downes Heath. NR32 — 17 E4
Downs Head St. NR32 — 14 C2
Drayton Dri. NR32 — 16 B2
Dulwich Way. NR32 — 16 C2
Duncan Rd. NR33 — 17 E3
Dunman Ct. NR33 — 18 C1

Eastern Way. NR33 — 17 E5
Edinfield Gdns. NR33 — 18 C3
Edgewood Av. NR33 — 19 E2
Edelweiss Clo. NR33 — 18 B3
Eskdale. NR32 — 15 D4
Elton Rd. NR33 — 19 E1
Edinburgh Rd. NR32 — 14 C1
Ellesmein Rd. NR32 — 19 F2
Elm Clo. NR33 — 16 D3
Elizabeth Clo. NR32 — 18 B5
Elmo. NR33 — 18 B5
Elm Coppice. NR33 — 18 D4
Englee Rd. NR33 — 18 D2
Englee Rd West. NR33 — 18 D2
Ennerdale Dri. NR32 — 18 C4
Everest Av. NR32 — 16 B4
Exe Rd. NR33 — 19 G1
Exe Way. NR32 — 16 D1
Eade. NR33 — 17 G6
Eden Rd. NR32 — 17 E4
Edd. NR32 — 14 A3
Edon Rd. NR32 — 17 F1
Exe Dri. NR32 — 17 E3
Fallen Rd. NR32 — 17 E3
Ferndale Ct. NR32 — 16 A5
Faraday Rd. NR33 — 16 B6
Ferry St. NR32 — 14 C2
Ferry Dri. NR33 — 18 C1
Ferry Rd. NR33 — 18 C1
Fennelds. NR32 — 12 D6
Fentley Rd. NR33 — 18 B5
Ferno. NR33 — 16 C2
Fern Clo. NR33 — 16 C2
Fern lo. NR33 — 19 F4
Fernham Ct. NR33 — 19 F4
Fern JR33 — 19 E2
Fern Cres. NR33 — 19 E2
Fern NR32 — 15 D4

Fern Green Clo. NR32 — 16 B2
Ferndale Av. NR32 — 17 E2
Fieldview Dri. NR32 — 17 E4
Fir La. NR32 — 16 D3
Fisher Row. NR32 — 15 B5
Fiske Gdns. NR32 — 16 C1
Fleet Dyke Rd. NR33 — 18 D3
Flensburgh St. NR32 — 14 B5
Flixton Marsh La. NR32 — 12 A5
Flixton Rd. NR32 — 12 A1
Flora Rd. NR32 — 19 E4
Florence Rd. NR32 — 19 F4
Fortress Rd. NR33 — 18 D4
Four Ways La. NR32 — 12 A1
Fowlers Cres. NR32 — 13 G2
Fox Glade. NR32 — 16 A4
Foxborough Rd. NR32 — 16 D1
Foxburrow Hill. NR32 — 13 E5
Foxglove Clo. NR33 — 15 C4
Framfield Clo. NR33 — 18 B4
Fritton Clo. NR32 — 16 C2
Frostenden Cres. NR32 — 17 E1
Fulmar Way. NR33 — 18 C2
Fyffe Way. NR33 — 14 B6

Gainsborough Dri. NR32 — 13 F5
Gasworks Rd. NR32 — 14 D3
Gilpin Rd. NR32 — 15 D4
Gladstone Rd. NR32 — 13 F2
Glebe Clo. NR32 — 17 F1
Glemsford Rd. NR32 — 16 C2
Glenbourne Wk. NR33 — 18 B4
Godetia Clo. NR32 — 17 E1
Gondree. NR33 — 18 D5
Gordon Rd. NR32 — 24 B4
Gorleston Rd. NR32 — 16 C4
Gorse Grn. NR32 — 17 E3
Grampian Way. NR32 — 15 D3
Grand Av. NR33 — 19 F4
Grange Rd. NR32 — 15 D3
Granville Rd. NR32 — 14 B4
Gravel Dam. NR32 — 15 A3
Grayson Av. NR33 — 19 F5
Grayson Dri. NR33 — 19 F5
Green Dri. NR33 — 19 F3
Green Fleet Dri. NR32 — 16 B2
Greenacre Cres. NR32 — 17 E3
Greenfield Rd. NR32 — 16 B2
Greenwood Way. NR32 — 13 G5
Gresham Av. NR32 — 16 C3
Gresham Clo. NR32 — 16 C3
Grosvenor Rd. NR33 — 17 F6
Grove Rd. NR32 — 14 C5
Grove Rd, Carlton Colville. NR32 — 18 B3
Gun La. NR32 — 14 C2
Gunton Av. NR32 — 13 E4
Gunton Church La. NR32 — 13 G6
Gunton Cliff. NR32 — 17 G1
Gunton Dri. NR32 — 13 H6
Gunton St Peters Av. NR32 — 17 F1
Guscott Clo. NR32 — 13 E6

Hadenham Rd. NR33 — 19 E6
Hadleigh Dri. NR32 — 16 C3
Hague Clo. NR32 — 18 B2
Halcyon Cres. NR32 — 17 F4
Hall Dri. NR32 — 15 C4
Hall La, Blundeston. NR32 — 12 B2
Hall La, Oulton. NR32 — 16 B1
Hall Rd, Blundeston. NR32 — 12 A4
Hall Rd, Carlton Colville. NR33 — 18 A5
Hall Rd, Oulton. NR33 — 16 A4
Hamilton Rd. NR32 — 14 D4
Harbour Rd. NR32 — 16 D6
Hardy Clo. NR33 — 16 D6
Harebell Way. NR33 — 18 C3
Harold Rd. NR33 — 19 G2
Harps Close Rd. NR32 — 17 E3
Harris Av. NR32 — 17 F1
Harrison Rd, NR32 — 16 B5
Harrison Rd, Pakefield. NR33 — 19 F5
*Harry Chamberlain Ct, Hopelyn Clo. NR32 — 17 E1

Harvest Dri. NR32 — 19 E5
Haven Av. NR32 — 17 E2
Haward St. NR32 — 14 A4
Hawthorn Av. NR32 — 19 E1
Healey Clo. NR32 — 13 E6
Heath La. NR32 — 12 A1
Heath Rd. NR32 — 16 D6
Heather Rd. NR32 — 17 G1
Hedley La. NR33 — 18 A4
Heigham Dri. NR33 — 19 E2
Henham Rd. NR32 — 17 E1
Herivan Gdns. NR32 — 16 B2
Herons Clo. NR32 — 15 D4
Herring Fishery Score. NR32 — 14 D3
Hervey St. NR32 — 14 A5
High Beech. NR32 — 17 E3
High St. NR32 — 14 C1
Higher Dri. NR32 — 16 C2
Highgrove Clo. NR32 — 16 D3
Highland Way. NR33 — 18 D1
Hildesley Clo. NR33 — 19 F4
Hill House Gdns. NR33 — 19 G2
Hill Rd. NR32 — 17 F4
Hillcrest Dri. NR32 — 17 E2
Hillcrest Gdns. NR32 — 17 E2
Hilltop Grn. NR32 — 17 E2
Hobart Clo. NR32 — 16 B2
Hobart Way. NR32 — 16 B2
Hogarth Walk. NR32 — 13 F6
Holbein Way. NR32 — 13 F5
Holbrook Rd. NR32 — 16 C2
Holden Clo. NR32 — 15 C4
Hollingsworth Rd. NR32 — 17 F2
Hollow Grove Way. NR33 — 18 B3
Hollow La. NR33 — 18 B3
Hollowell Clo. NR32 — 16 B2
Holly Rd. NR32 — 16 B5
Hollydene Clo. NR32 — 15 C3
Holme Ct. NR32 — 15 C3
Holst Clo. NR33 — 19 F2
Holton Av. NR32 — 16 C2
Homefield Av. NR33 — 19 E2
Honeysuckle Clo. NR33 — 19 E5
Hopelyn Clo. NR32 — 17 E1
Horn Hill. NR33 — 17 F6
Houghton Dri. NR32 — 16 B1
Howley Gdns. NR32 — 13 E5
Hubbards Av. NR32 — 13 G5
Hubbards Loke. NR32 — 13 G5
Huntingdon Clo. NR33 — 19 F5

INDUSTRIAL & RETAIL:
Beach Ind Est. NR32 — 17 H3
Oulton Ind Est. NR32 — 16 B2
South Lowestoft Ind Est. NR33 — 19 E6
Ipswich Rd. NR32 — 14 B1
Irex Rd. NR33 — 19 F4
Ivy La. NR33 — 18 B1

Jacobs Ct. NR32 — 14 B3
Jacobs St. NR32 — 14 B3
Jasmine Grn. NR32 — 17 F3
Jeannie Mann Ct. NR32 — 17 E2
Jellicoe Av. NR33 — 18 C2
Jenkins Grn. NR32 — 13 E6
John Lang Ct. NR33 — 16 B6
John St. NR33 — 19 G1
Johnson Way. NR32 — 13 E6
Jubilee Rd. NR33 — 19 F6
Jubilee Way. NR32 — 14 C2
June Av. NR32 — 17 E3
Katwijk Way. NR32 — 14 B4
Keel Clo. NR33 — 18 A4
Kelly Pain Ct. NR32 — 17 F2
Kelsale Clo. NR32 — 16 D2
Kendal Rd. NR33 — 19 G3
Kensington Rd. NR33 — 19 G2
Kent Rd. NR32 — 17 E4
Kesgrave Dri. NR32 — 16 C3
Kestral Grn. NR33 — 18 B2
Kevington Dri. NR32 — 15 C4
Kilbourn Rd. NR32 — 19 E5
Kimberley Rd. NR33 — 16 D6
Kingfisher Ct. NR33 — 18 B2
Kingston Clo. NR33 — 19 F4
Kingswood Av. NR33 — 18 C3

Kirby Cane Wk. NR32 — 16 D3
Kirkdale Ct. NR33 — 19 G4
Kirkley Cliff. NR33 — 19 H1
Kirkley Cliff Rd. NR33 — 19 G2
Kirkley Gdns. NR33 — 19 F2
Kirkley Park Rd. NR33 — 19 G2
Kirkley Run. NR33 — 19 F1
Kirkley St. NR33 — 19 G1
Kirkstone Way. NR32 — 16 D1
Kirkwood Dri. NR33 — 18 B4
Kittiwake Clo. NR33 — 18 C2
Knights Wood. NR32 — 13 F6
Lake View Rd. NR33 — 16 C6
Lakeland Dri. NR32 — 16 C4
Lakeside Rise. NR32 — 12 A4
Landspring La. NR33 — 18 D2
Langdale Pk. NR32 — 16 C4
Langley Gdns. NR33 — 19 E2
Lansdowne Rd. NR33 — 19 E4
Larch Rd. NR32 — 17 E3
Larkspur Clo. NR32 — 13 F4
Lattens Sq. NR32 — 14 A3
Laurel Rd. NR32 — 19 G2
Lavenham Way. NR32 — 16 D3
Lawrence Dri. NR32 — 13 F5
Lawson Rd. NR33 — 19 H1
Laxfield Way. NR33 — 19 E4
Leas Drift. NR33 — 18 B2
Leathes Clo. NR32 — 16 C4
Leiston Rd. NR32 — 14 C3
Leisure Way. NR32 — 13 E5
Leona Cres. NR33 — 18 B4
Leonard Dri. NR32 — 13 E5
Lighthouse Score. NR32 — 17 H2
Lilac Dri. NR32 — 17 E3
Lily Way. NR33 — 18 B3
Lime Av. NR32 — 15 D3
Lime Clo. NR32 — 15 D3
Links Clo. NR33 — 19 E3
Links Rd. NR32 — 13 H6
London Rd. NR33 — 19 F5
London Rd Nth. NR32 — 14 C5
London Rd Sth. NR33 — 19 F4
Long Acre. NR32 — 19 G4
Long Fields Path. NR32 — 16 B2
Long Meadow Wk. NR33 — 18 C3
Long Rd. NR33 — 18 D4
Longbeach Dri. NR33 — 18 C5
Longboat Clo. NR32 — 16 C4
Longfield Way. NR32 — 15 D3
Lorne Park Rd. NR33 — 19 G1
Lorne Rd. NR33 — 19 G1
Lothing St. NR32 — 16 C5
Lound Rd. NR32 — 12 A1
Love La. NR33 — 19 E4
Love Rd. NR32 — 14 A3
Lovewell Rd. NR32 — 19 G1
Low Farm Dri. NR33 — 18 B5
Lowestoft Rd. NR32 — 12 B3
Lowestoft Rd. NR33 — 18 C4
Lowry Way. NR32 — 13 G6
Loxley Rd. NR33 — 18 D1
Lucerne Clo. NR33 — 18 B3
Lulworth Pk. NR32 — 16 D2
Lupton Rd. NR32 — 17 E1
Lyncroft Rd. NR32 — 19 G4
Lyndhurst Rd. NR32 — 17 G2
Lyngate Av. NR32 — 18 D3
Lynton Gdns. NR32 — 17 F2

Magdalen Clo. NR32 — 16 D2
Magnolia Ct. NR32 — 17 E3
Maidstone Rd. NR32 — 14 A5
Mallow Way. NR33 — 18 B3
Maltsters Score. NR32 — 14 D3
Maltsters Rd. NR32 — 16 A5
Malvern Rise. NR32 — 17 E2
Manor Ct. NR32 — 14 C3
Manor Park Rd. NR32 — 13 F2
Mantis Cres. NR32 — 17 E1
Maple Clo. NR32 — 19 E1
Marbella Grn. NR33 — 18 C3
Marham Rd. NR32 — 17 F3
Marina. NR32 — 14 C5
Marine Par. NR32 — 17 G6
Mariners Score. NR32 — 14 C3
Market La. NR32 — 12 B2
Marlborough Ct. NR32 — 16 C4
Marlborough Rd. NR32 — 16 C4
Marsden Clo. NR33 — 19 E5

Marsh La. NR33 — 18 A3
Marsh Rd. NR33 — 16 B6
Marshalls Piece. NR33 — 18 B2
Mast Clo. NR33 — 18 A4
Martello Rd. NR32 — 17 E1
Martin Clo. NR33 — 18 C5
Martins Av. NR33 — 19 G1
Martins Score. NR32 — 14 D2
Matlowck Dale. NR33 — 18 D5
Mautby Way. NR33 — 19 E3
May Rd. NR32 — 14 A4
Mayfield Rd. NR33 — 18 B4
Meadow Rd. NR32 — 16 C1
Meadow Way. NR33 — 18 B5
Meadowlands. NR32 — 12 B1
Meadowsweet Clo. NR33 — 18 C3
Melbourne Rd. NR32 — 14 B1
Melrose Clo. NR32 — 16 C1
Mendip Rd. NR32 — 16 B3
Merrifield Rd. NR33 — 19 E4
Merville. NR33 — 18 D5
Mews Ct. NR32 — 16 D1
Middle Way. NR32 — 13 G6
Mill Bank. NR32 — 16 C3
Mill La. NR32 — 13 G2
Mill Rd. NR33 — 17 F6
Miller Clo. NR33 — 19 F2
Mills Dri. NR32 — 13 G3
Milton Rd East. NR32 — 14 C3
Milton Rd West. NR32 — 14 B3
Mimosa Wk. NR32 — 17 E3
Minden Rd. NR32 — 14 A3
Minos Rd. NR32 — 17 F1
Mobbs Way. NR32 — 16 B3
Monckton Av. NR32 — 16 D3
Monckton Cres. NR32 — 16 D4
Monet Sq. NR32 — 13 F6
Monkshood Clo. NR33 — 19 E5
Montgomery Av. NR32 — 17 E2
Morton Rd. NR33 — 19 G3
Mount Pleasant. NR32 — 17 F2
Mountbatten Rd. NR32 — 17 E1
Moyes Rd. NR32 — 15 D4
Munnings Clo. NR33 — 18 B4
Murillo Dri. NR32 — 13 G6
Mutford Clo. NR32 — 16 C4
Mutfordwood La. NR33 — 18 A5
Mylodon Rd. NR32 — 17 F1
Myrtle Clo. NR32 — 17 E3

Nelson Rd. NR33 — 19 F4
Nelson Way. NR33 — 16 C6
Neptune St. NR32 — 17 F5
Newark Rd. NR32 — 19 G1
Newcombe Ct. NR32 — 16 A3
Newcombe Rd. NR32 — 14 D4
Newlands Clo. NR33 — 19 E4
Newsons Mdw. NR32 — 17 F3
Nicholson Sq. NR32 — 14 A3
Nidderdale. NR33 — 18 D5
Nightingale Rd. NR33 — 19 G4
Ninfield Clo. NR33 — 18 C4
Noel Rd. NR32 — 15 C4
Norfolk St. NR32 — 17 E4
Normandy Rd. NR32 — 17 E1
Normanshurst Clo. NR32 — 16 D3
Normanston Dri. NR32 — 16 C4
North Denes Sea Wall. NR32 — 17 H2
North Par. NR32 — 17 G2
Northfield Clo. NR32 — 12 D6
Northgate. NR32 — 17 E3
Northwood Clo. NR33 — 19 E2
Norwich Rd. NR32 — 14 A4
Notley Rd. NR33 — 19 F1

Oakwood Rd. NR33 — 19 E2
Oatlands Clo. NR33 — 18 C3
Ohio Clo. NR33 — 18 D4
Old Farm Rd. NR33 — 18 C3
Old La. NR32 — 13 F4
Old Market Sq. NR32 — 14 C3
Old Nelson St. NR32 — 14 C4
Olive Ct. NR32 — 17 E3
Oliver Clo. NR33 — 18 C5
Ontario Rd. NR33 — 19 G1
Orchard Av. NR33 — 18 D1
Orchard Clo. NR32 — 12 B1
Orchard Croft. NR33 — 18 C3

Orchard La. NR32 12 B2
Orford Dri. NR32 16 C2
Orwell Dri. NR32 16 D2
Osborne St. NR32 14 C1
Osprey Grn. NR33 18 C2
Oulton Ct. NR32 16 B2
Oulton Rd,
 Blundeston. NR32 12 D3
Oulton Rd,
 Lowestoft. NR32 17 E3
Oulton St. NR32 16 C1
Oxford Rd. NR32 14 B1

Paddock Hill. NR33 18 D1
Paddock Wood Clo.
 NR33 18 B4
Pakefield. NR33 19 F4
Pakefield Rd. NR33 19 G2
Pakefield St. NR33 19 G4
Palmer Clo. NR32 13 F5
Parade Rd Nth. NR3 14 B6
Parade Rd Sth. NR33 17 G6
Park Clo. NR33 18 C3
Park Rd. NR32 14 C2
Parkhill. NR32 12 D6
Parkholme Ter. NR32 17 G2
Parkside Dri. NR32 16 D4
Patricia Clo. NR32 15 D4
Patterdale Gdns.
 NR32 16 D1
Payne St. NR32
Peacock Clo. NR33 18 B5
Peak Dale. NR33 18 D5
Pebble Clo. NR32 16 D2
Peddars Way. NR32 17 E2
Pegasus Mws. NR32 16 B5
Pembroke Way. NR32 16 D2
Pennine Way. NR32 16 C3
Pennygate Dri. NR33 18 D2
Pentland Wk. NR32 16 D2
Periwinkle Clo. NR33 18 B3
Peto Way. NR32 16 D1
Pier Ter. NR32 17 G6
Pinbush Clo. NR32 18 D5
Pinbush Rd. NR33 19 E5
Pinewood Av. NR33 19 E2
Planters Gro. NR33 19 E1
Pleasurewood Hill.
 NR32 13 E4
Plovers Way. NR33 15 C4
Plumtrees. NR32
Police Station Rd.
 NR32 14 C4
Pollard Piece. NR32 18 B2
Poplar Rd. NR33 18 C4
Porthole Clo. NR33 18 A4
Portcull Clo. NR33 18 D4
Pound Farm Dri.
 NR32 16 C2
Pound La. NR32 12 D3
Primrose Clo. NR33 19 E5
Princes Rd. NR32 14 A2
Princes Wk. NR32 16 D4
Priors Clo. NR32 13 F6
Privet Grn. NR33 19 E1
Prospect Pl. NR33 19 G4
Prospect Rd. NR32 15 B5

Queens Highway.
 NR32 15 B4
Queens Rd. NR32 14 C1
Quinnell Way. NR32 13 E5

Raglan Rd. NR32 14 B3
Raglan St. NR32 14 B2
Rant Score. NR32 14 D3
Ranville. NR33 18 D5
Ranworth Av. NR33 18 D2
Raphael Walk. NR32 13 F6
Rectory Rd, Carlton
 Colville. NR33 18 B5

Rectory Rd,
 Lowestoft. NR33 19 G2
Red House Clo. NR32 16 C1
Redisham Clo. NR32 13 E6
Reeve St. NR32 14 B2
Regan Clo. NR32 13 E6
Regent Rd. NR32 14 C4
Rembrandt Clo. NR32 13 G6
Renoir Pl. NR32 13 F6
Reydon Mews. NR32 13 E6
Reynolds Walk. NR32 13 F6
Ribblesdale. NR33 18 D4
Richmond Rd. NR33 19 H1
Ridgeville. NR33 19 E5
Ringsfield Rd. NR32 16 D3
Rio Clo. NR33 18 B2
Rishton Rd. NR32 14 B4
Rivendale. NR33 18 C5
Riverside Rd. NR33 17 E6
Robertsbridge Way.
 NR33 18 C4
Robin Hill. NR32 17 E4
Rochdale. NR33 19 E5
Rochester Rd. NR33 19 G3
Rock Rd. NR32 15 D4
Rodber Way. NR32 13 E6
Roman Rd. NR32 14 A4
Romany Rd. NR32 15 C5
Romney Pl. NR32 13 F6
Rookery Clo. NR33 16 C6
Roosevelt Wk. NR33 18 B2
Rose Ct. NR32 17 E3
Rosedale Clo. NR33 18 D4
Rosedale Gdns. NR33 18 D4
Rosewood. NR33 19 E2
Rotterdam Rd. NR32 17 F3
Rounces La. NR33 18 B4
Rowan Way. NR33 18 C2
Royal Av. NR32 17 G2
Royal Ter. NR33 17 G6
Roydon Way. NR32 16 C1
Rozlyne Clo. NR33 18 D4
*Rubens Walk, Sutherland
 Dri. NR32 13 F6
Ruby Clo. NR33 13 G3
Rumburgh Rd. NR32 17 E1
Run Mdw. NR33 18 B2
Rushlake Way. NR33 18 C4
Rushmere Rd. NR33 18 B6
Rye Clo. NR33 18 C3
Ryedale. NR33 18 D4

Saffron Sq. NR33 19 E5
St Catherines Clo.
 NR33 18 D3
St Georges Rd. NR33 19 G3
St Johns Rd. NR33 17 F6
St Leonards Rd. NR33 19 G1
St Margarets Plain.
 NR32 14 C2
St Margarets Rd.
 NR32 14 A1
St Michaels Clo. NR32 15 C4
*St Peters Ct,
 St Peters St. NR32 14 C2
St Peters Rd, Carlton
 Colville. NR33 18 B4
St Peters Rd,
 Lowestoft. NR33 19 G2
St Peters St. NR32 14 C2
St Quintons Clo. NR33 19 F3
Salisbury St. NR33 19 G1
Saltwater Way. NR33 16 B5
San Francisco Wk.
 NR33 18 B2
Sanctuary Gdns. NR32 16 C1
Sandbank Rd. NR33 18 D3
Sanders Clo. NR32 16 C2
Sandringham Rd.
 NR32 17 F4
Sands La. NR32 16 A3
Saturn Clo. NR33 17 G1
Saxon Clo. NR33 19 F4

School Rd. NR33 16 C6
Scroby Ct. NR32 15 C3
Seago St. NR32 14 B4
Seavert Clo. NR33 18 D4
Sedlescombe Rd.
 NR33 18 C3
Selby St. NR32 17 F5
Shadingfield Clo.
 NR32 13 E6
Sharon Dri. NR32 17 E2
Shaw Av. NR33 18 C5
Shelton Rd. NR33 19 E5
Ship Rd. NR33 19 E4
Shoals Wk. NR33 18 D2
Short La. NR33 18 B5
Short Rd. NR32 12 B2
Short St. NR33 19 G3
Silverwood Clo. NR33 19 H4
Siskin Grn. NR33 18 C2
Skamacre Cres. NR32 17 F4
Skoulding Clo. NR33 16 C6
Smiths Wk. NR33 18 B1
Snape Dri. NR32 16 D2
Somerleyton Rd,
 Lowestoft. NR32 16 C1
Somerleyton Rd,
 Somerleyton. NR32 12 A3
Somerton Av. NR32 14 A1
Sotterley Clo. NR32 13 E6
Sotterley Rd. NR32 16 D2
South Elmham Ter.
 NR33 16 B6
South Leet Clo. NR31 16 B2
South View Clo.
 NR32 17 E4
Southfield Gdns.
 NR33 19 E2
Southwell Rd. NR33 19 G1
Spashett Rd. NR32 17 E1
Speedwell Clo. NR33 19 E5
Spencer Dri. NR32 13 F6
Spexall Way. NR32 17 E1
Springfield Gdns.
 NR33 19 E2
Spruce Ct. NR33 17 F3
Spurgeon Score.
 NR32 14 D3
Squires Walk. NR33 13 G6
Stafford Ct. NR32 16 C2
Stanford St. NR32 14 A4
Stanley Rd. NR33 16 C6
Stanley St. NR32 14 B4
Stansfield Clo. NR33 18 D1
Stanton Clo. NR32 13 E6
Staplehurst Clo. NR33 18 B4
Station Rd,
 Corton. NR32 13 G2
Station Rd,
 Lowestoft. NR32 17 G2
Station Sq. NR32 17 G5
Stayngate Wk. NR32 16 B2
Stephensons Wk.
 NR32 17 G1
Stevens Clo. NR32 17 F5
Stimpson Clo. NR33 13 E5
Stirling Clo. NR32 16 C1
Stirrups La. NR32 12 D1
Stoven Clo. NR32 17 E1
Stradbroke Rd. NR33 18 C5
Stubbs Wood. NR32 13 F5
Suffolk Rd. NR32 14 C5
Summer Rd. NR32 14 B4
Summerfield Gdns.
 NR33 19 E2
Sunningdale Av.
 NR33 19 G4
Sunny Fields. NR33 18 D6
Surrey St. NR32 14 B5
Sussex Rd. NR32 17 G2
Sutherland Dri. NR32 13 F5
Swallowfields. NR33 14 A5
Swift Clo. NR33 18 C4
Swonnells Wk. NR32 16 A5

Sycamore Av. NR33 18 C1
Tansy Clo. NR33 19 E5
Tedder Rd. NR32 17 E2
Teesdale. NR33 18 D5
Telesia Ct. NR32 17 E1
Tennyson Rd. NR32 14 C3
Tenterden Clo. NR33 18 B5
The Avenue. NR33 19 F2
The Boulevard. NR33 16 B5
The Brindles. NR33 18 D4
The Close. NR32 13 G2
The Cut. NR32 13 G2
The Drive. NR32 16 C3
The Eddies. NR33 18 D3
The Fairway. NR33 18 B5
The Firs. NR33 18 B5
The Gap. NR33 19 E1
The Gardens. NR33 18 B6
The Glades. NR33 15 D4
The Green. NR33 19 E1
The Greylings. NR33 18 C4
The Hemplands. NR32 14 C1
The Leas. NR32 12 D6
The Loke. NR32 12 D6
The Meads. NR32 17 F1
The Parklands. NR33 18 C3
The Pastures. NR32 12 D6
The Pippins. NR32 12 B1
The Prarie. NR32 14 C5
The Ravine. NR32 17 G2
The Ridgeways. NR33 18 C3
The Shires. NR33 13 F4
The Sound. NR33 18 D3
The Staithe. NR33 18 D2
The Street,
 Blundeston. NR32 12 B1
The Street,
 Corton. NR32 13 G2
The Street,
 Oulton. NR33 16 B5
The Trossachs. NR32 15 D3
The Venlaw. NR33 19 G2
The Weald. NR32 16 B3
The Woodlands. NR32 13 F4
Thirlmere Wk. NR32 16 D2
Thistledown. NR33 18 C3
Thornham Clo. NR33 19 E4
Thurne Rd. NR33 19 E2
Thurston Rd. NR32 14 C2
Till Rd. NR32 14 B4
Tonning St. NR32 14 A5
Tower Rd. NR33 19 E6
Trafalgar St. NR32 14 A5
Tramps Alley. NR32 13 H4
*Triangle Yd,
 St Peters St. NR32 14 C3
Trinity Rd. NR32 13 G2
Tudor Wk. NR32 18 D4
Tunstall Dri. NR32 16 C2
Turnberry Clo. NR33 19 E3
Turner Clo. NR32 13 F6

Ubbeston Way. NR33 19 E4
Uggeshall Clo. NR32 16 D1
Ullswater. NR33 18 C5
Union La. NR33 16 C1
Union Pl. NR33 19 H1
Union Rd. NR32 14 A4
Uplands Clo. NR33 18 C3
Uplands Rd Sth.
 NR33 18 B4
Uplands Rd Nth.
 NR33 18 C3
Upper Esplanade.
 NR33 19 H2

Vallibus Clo. NR32 16 B2
Van Dyke Clo. NR32 13 F6
Velda Clo. NR33 18 D4
Verdure Clo. NR32 12 D6
Vermeer Clo. NR32 13 F5
Viburnum Grn. NR32 17 F3

Victoria Rd. NR33 16 B
Village Way. NR32 13 F
Wainwright Clo. NR32 13 E
Walberswick Way.
 NR32 16 D
Walcott Wk. NR33 19 F
Walmer Rd. NR33 19 F
Walton Rd. NR32 14 A
Wannock Clo. NR32 18 C
Warren La. NR32 12 A
Warren Rd. NR32 17 G
Water La. NR32 14 A
Waters Av. NR33 18 B
Waveney Cres. NR33 17 C
Waveney Dri. NR33 16 D
Waveney Hill. NR32 15 B
Waveney Rd. NR32 14
Wayne Clo. NR32 13
Wedgewood Ct.
 NR32 17
Wellington Esp.
 NR33 19
Wellington Rd. NR33 19
Wenhaston Way.
 NR32 16
Wensleydale. NR33 18
Wentworth Way.
 NR33 19
Wesley St. NR32 14
West Gro. NR33 19
West Side Clo. NR33 13
Westhall Rd. NR32 16
Westland Rd. NR33 18
Weston Rd. NR32 17
Westwood Av. NR33 18
Whapload Rd. NR32 14
Wharfdale. NR33 18
Wheatacre Dri. NR32 13
Wheatfield Rd. NR33 18
*Whinland Wk, Breckland
 Way. NR32 16
Whiskin Clo. NR32 16
White Horse St. NR32 1
Whiting Rd. NR32 1
Whitton Clo. NR33 1
Whitton Ct. NR33
Wiggs Way. NR32
Wildes Score. NR32 1
Wildes St. NR32 1
Willow Rd. NR33
Wilson Rd. NR33
Windermere Pk.
 NR32
Windsor Rd. NR33
Windward Way. NR33
Winnipeg Rd. NR32
Winston Av. NR33
Wissett Way. NR32
Witney Green. NR33
Witney Rd. NR33
Wollaston Rd. NR32
Wood La. NR32
Woodlands. NR33
Woodpecker Av.
 NR33
Woods Loke E. NR32
Woods Loke W. NR32
Woodside Clo. NR33
Worlingham Way.
 NR32
Worthing Rd. NR32

Yarmouth Rd,
 Corton. NR32
Yarmouth Rd,
 Lowestoft. NR32
Yarrow Dri. NR33
Yeovil Rd. NR32
Yew Dale. NR33
York Rd. NR32